EASY CHRISTMAS PIANO SOLOS

ARRANGED BY KEVIN OLSON

ISBN 978-1-70514-125-0

For all works contained herein:
Unauthorized copying, arranging, adapting, recording, internet posting, public performance,
or other distribution of the music in this publication is an infringement of copyright.
Infringers are liable under the law.

Visit Hal Leonard Online at
www.halleonard.com

Contact us:
Hal Leonard
7777 West Bluemound Road
Milwaukee, WI 53213
Email: info@halleonard.com

In Europe, contact:
Hal Leonard Europe Limited
42 Wigmore Street
Marylebone, London, W1U 2RN
Email: info@halleonardeurope.com

In Australia, contact:
Hal Leonard Australia Pty. Ltd.
4 Lentara Court
Cheltenham, Victoria, 3192 Australia
Email: info@halleonard.com.au

PREFACE

Some of my earliest Christmas memories are sitting around a big record player console at my parents' house with the lights dimmed, listening to scratchy LPs of Christmas standards by Nat King Cole, Burl Ives, the Carpenters, Mannheim Steamroller, and others. When those same arrangements come over the speakers at grocery stores or my car speakers at Christmastime today, I still get that same nostalgic feeling of being a kid counting the days until Christmas morning. I hope this collection of Christmas classics, old and new, add to the spirit of the season for you and the family and friends who will listen to you play them. Best wishes for a joy-filled, musical Christmas season!

CONTENTS

ALL I WANT FOR CHRISTMAS IS YOU

Words and Music by MARIAH CAREY
and WALTER AFANASIEFF
Arranged by Kevin Olson

Dramatic and freely (♩ = 108)

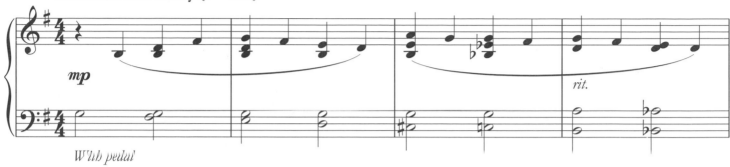

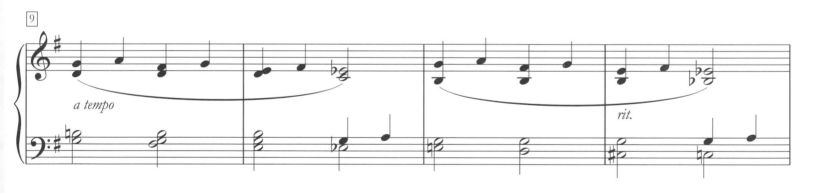

Copyright © 1994 UNIVERSAL TUNES, BEYONDIDOLIZATION, SONY MUSIC PUBLISHING LLC, TAMAL VISTA MUSIC and KOBALT MUSIC COPYRIGHTS SARL
All Rights for BEYONDIDOLIZATION Administered by UNIVERSAL TUNES
All Rights for SONY MUSIC PUBLISHING LLC and TAMAL VISTA MUSIC Administered by SONY MUSIC PUBLISHING LLC, 424 Church Street, Suite 1200, Nashville, TN 37219
All Rights for KOBALT MUSIC COPYRIGHTS SARL Administered Worldwide by KOBALT SONGS MUSIC PUBLISHING
All Rights Reserved   Used by Permission

CHRISTMAS LIGHTS

Words and Music by GUY BERRYMAN,
WILL CHAMPION, CHRIS MARTIN
and JONNY BUCKLAND
Arranged by Kevin Olson

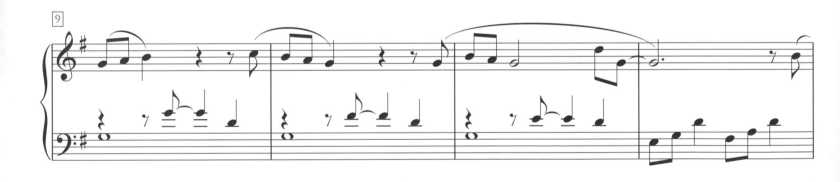

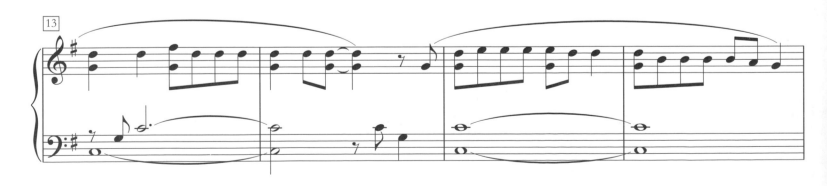

Copyright © 2010 by Universal Music Publishing MGB Ltd.
All Rights in the United States and Canada Administered by Universal Music - MGB Songs
International Copyright Secured   All Rights Reserved

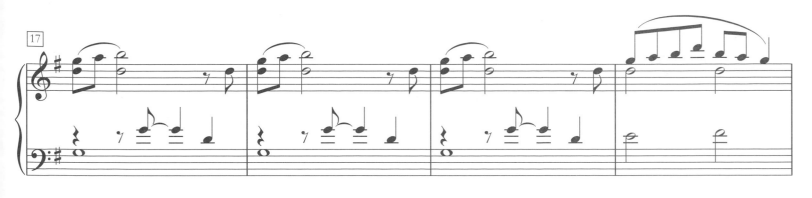

THE CHRISTMAS SONG
(Chestnuts Roasting on an Open Fire)

Music and Lyric by MEL TORMÉ
and ROBERT WELLS
Arranged by Kevin Olson

Slow Jazz Ballad

© 1946 (Renewed) EDWIN H. MORRIS & COMPANY, A Division of MPL Music Publishing, Inc. and SONY MUSIC PUBLISHING LLC
All Rights on behalf of SONY MUSIC PUBLISHING LLC Administered by SONY MUSIC PUBLISHING LLC, 424 Church Street, Suite 1200, Nashville, TN 37219
All Rights Reserved

COLD DECEMBER NIGHT

Words and Music by MICHAEL BUBLÉ,
ALAN CHANG and ROBERT ROCK
Arranged by Kevin Olson

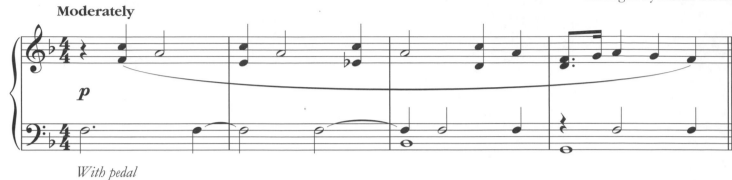

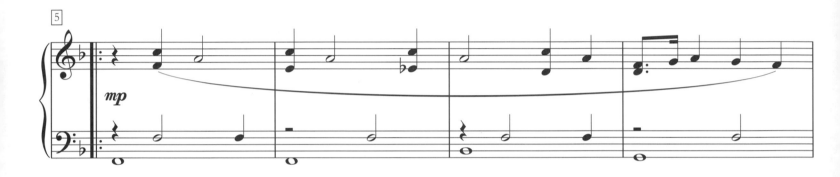

© 2011 I'M THE LAST MAN STANDING MUSIC, INC., IHAN ZHAN MUSIC, EMI BLACKWOOD MUSIC (CANADA) LTD. and MAHINA HOKU PUBLISHING
All Rights for I'M THE LAST MAN STANDING MUSIC, INC. Administered by WC MUSIC CORP.
All Rights for IHAN ZHAN MUSIC Administered by WARNER-TAMERLANE PUBLISHING CORP.
All Rights for EMI BLACKWOOD MUSIC (CANADA) LTD. and MAHINA HOKU PUBLISHING Administered by
SONY MUSIC PUBLISHING LLC, 424 Church Street, Suite 1200, Nashville, TN 37219
All Rights Reserved   Used by Permission

GROWN-UP CHRISTMAS LIST

Words and Music by DAVID FOSTER
and LINDA THOMPSON-JENNER
Arranged by Kevin Olson

Slow Pop feel

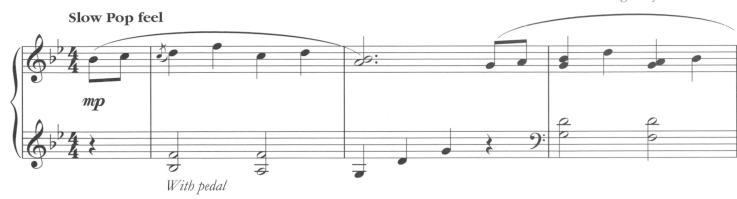

Copyright © 1990 by Air Bear Music, Warner-Tamerlane Publishing Corp. and Linda's Boys Music
All Rights for Air Bear Music Administered by Peermusic Ltd.
All Rights for Linda's Boys Music Administered by Warner-Tamerlane Publishing Corp.
International Copyright Secured   All Rights Reserved

DO YOU HEAR WHAT I HEAR

Words and Music by NOEL REGNEY
and GLORIA SHAYNE
Arranged by Kevin Olson

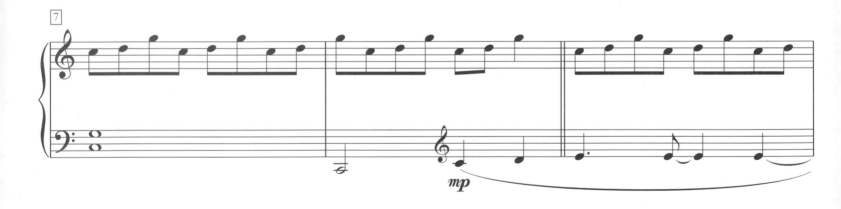

Copyright © 1962 (Renewed) by Jewel Music Publishing Co., Inc. (ASCAP)
International Copyright Secured   All Rights Reserved
Used by Permission

HAVE YOURSELF A MERRY LITTLE CHRISTMAS

from MEET ME IN ST. LOUIS

Words and Music by HUGH MARTIN
and RALPH BLANE
Arranged by Kevin Olson

© 1943 (Renewed) METRO-GOLDWYN-MAYER INC.
© 1944 (Renewed) EMI FEIST CATALOG INC.
All Rights Controlled and Administered by EMI FEIST CATALOG INC. (Publishing) and ALFRED MUSIC (Print)
All Rights Reserved   Used by Permission

IT'S BEGINNING TO LOOK LIKE CHRISTMAS

By MEREDITH WILLSON
Arranged by Kevin Olson

© 1951 PLYMOUTH MUSIC CO., INC.
© Renewed 1979 FRANK MUSIC CORP. and MEREDITH WILLSON MUSIC
All Rights Reserved

To Coda

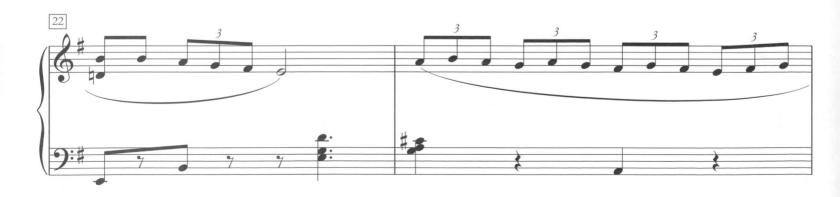

D.S. al Coda

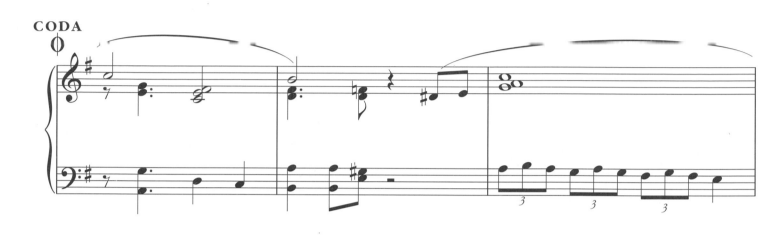

CODA

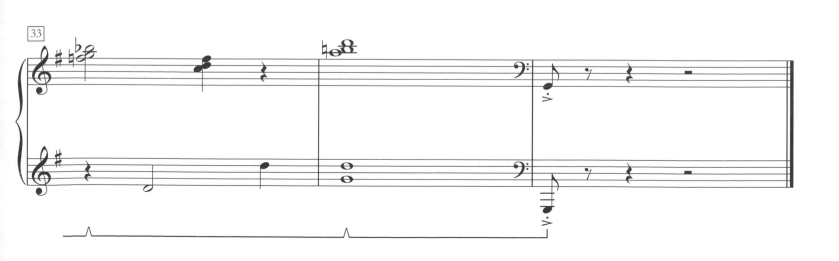

I'LL BE HOME FOR CHRISTMAS

Words and Music by KIM GANNON
and WALTER KENT
Arranged by Kevin Olson

Slow Swing feel

© Copyright 1943 by Gannon & Kent Music Co., Inc., Beverly Hills, CA
Copyright Renewed
International Copyright Secured   All Rights Reserved

THE MOST WONDERFUL
TIME OF THE YEAR

Words and Music by EDDIE POLA
and GEORGE WYLE
Arranged by Kevin Olson

Quick Jazz Waltz

Copyright © 1963 Barnaby Music Corp.
Copyright Renewed
Administered by Lichelle Music Company
International Copyright Secured   All Rights Reserved

LAST CHRISTMAS

Words and Music by
GEORGE MICHAEL
Arranged by Kevin Olson

Medium Pop feel

With pedal

© 1984 WHAM MUSIC LIMITED
All Rights Administered by WC MUSIC CORP.
All Rights Reserved   Used by Permission

LET IT SNOW! LET IT SNOW! LET IT SNOW!

Words by SAMMY CAHN
Music by JULE STYNE
Arranged by Kevin Olson

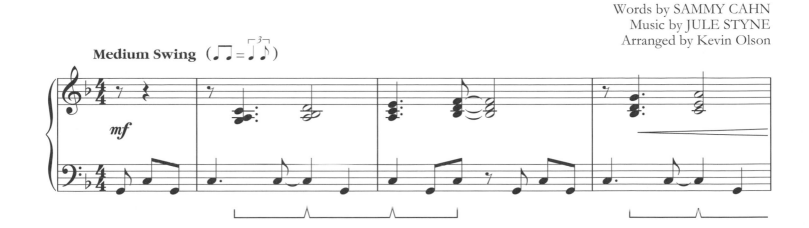

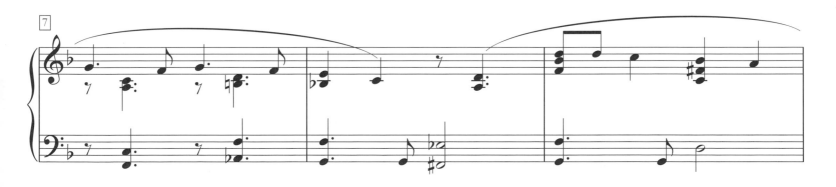

© 1945 (Renewed) PRODUCERS MUSIC PUBLISHING CO., INC. and CAHN MUSIC COMPANY
All Rights for PRODUCERS MUSIC PUBLISHING CO., INC. Administered by CHAPPELL & CO., INC.
All Rights for CAHN MUSIC COMPANY Administered by CONCORD SOUNDS c/o CONCORD MUSIC PUBLISHING
All Rights Reserved   Used by Permission

No pedal

THE LITTLE DRUMMER BOY

Words and Music by HARRY SIMEONE,
HENRY ONORATI and KATHERINE DAVIS
Arranged by Kevin Olson

Medium Rock beat

© 1958 (Renewed) EMI MILLS MUSIC, INC. and INTERNATIONAL KORWIN CORP.
Worldwide Print Rights Administered by ALFRED MUSIC
All Rights Reserved   Used by Permission

MISTLETOE

Words and Music by JUSTIN BIEBER,
NASRI ATWEH and ADAM MESSINGER
Arranged by Kevin Olson

Copyright © 2011 UNIVERSAL MUSIC CORP., BIEBER TIME PUBLISHING, SONY MUSIC PUBLISHING LLC, TRE BALL MUSIC and MESSY MUSIC
All Rights for BIEBER TIME PUBLISHING Controlled and Administered by UNIVERSAL MUSIC CORP.
All Rights for SONY MUSIC PUBLISHING LLC and TRE BALL MUSIC Administered by SONY MUSIC PUBLISHING LLC, 424 Church Street, Suite 1200, Nashville, TN 37219
All Rights Reserved   Used by Permission

ROCKIN' AROUND
THE CHRISTMAS TREE

Music and Lyrics by
JOHNNY MARKS
Arranged by Kevin Olson

Up-tempo Rock

Copyright © 1958 (Renewed 1986) St. Nicholas Music Inc., 254 W. 54th Street, 12th Floor, New York, New York 10019
All Rights Reserved

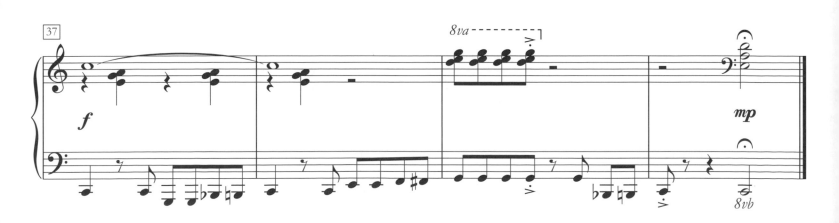

SANTA BABY

By JOAN JAVITS, PHIL SPRINGER
and TONY SPRINGER
Arranged by Kevin Olson

© 1953 Trinity Music, Inc.
Copyright Renewed 1981 and Controlled in the U.S. by Philip Springer
Copyright Controlled for the world outside the U.S. by Alley Music Corp. and Trio Music Company
All Rights for Trio Music Company Administered by BMG Rights Management (US) LLC
International Copyright Secured   All Rights Reserved

SANTA CLAUS IS COMIN' TO TOWN

Words by HAVEN GILLESPIE
Music by J. FRED COOTS
Arranged by Kevin Olson

Copyright © 1934 Toy Town Tunes, Inc. and Haven Gillespie Music
Copyright Renewed
All Rights on behalf of Toy Town Tunes, Inc. Administered in the United States and Canada by Wixen Music Publishing, Inc.
All Rights Reserved   Used by Permission

SANTA, TELL ME

Words and Music by SAVAN KOTECHA,
ILYA and ARIANA GRANDE
Arranged by Kevin Olson

Medium Pop

Copyright © 2013, 2014 MXM, BMG Gold Songs, Warner Chappell Music Scandinavia AB, Wolf Cousins and Grandarimusic
All Rights for MXM Administered Worldwide by Kobalt Songs Music Publishing
All Rights for BMG Gold Songs Administered by BMG Rights Management (US) LLC
All Rights for Warner Chappell Music Scandinavia AB and Wolf Cousins in the U.S. and Canada Administered by WC Music Corp.
All Rights for Grandarimusic Administered by Universal Music Corp.
All Rights Reserved   Used by Permission

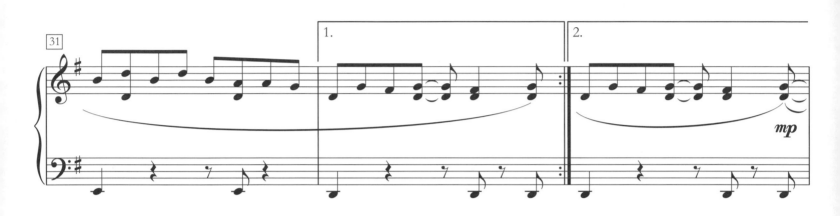

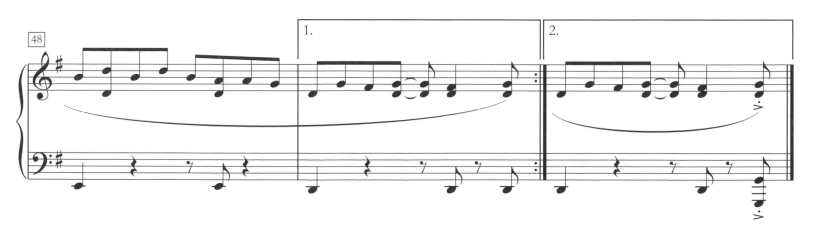

WHAT ARE YOU DOING NEW YEAR'S EVE?

By FRANK LOESSER
Arranged by Kevin Olson

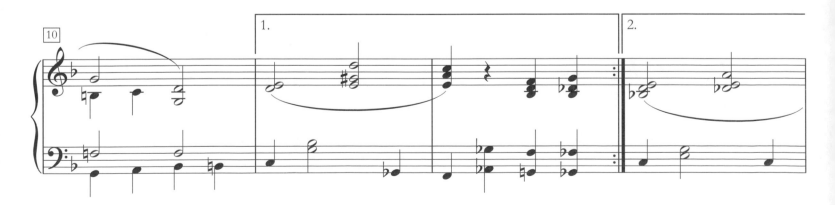

© 1947 (Renewed) FRANK MUSIC CORP.
All Rights Reserved

WHITE CHRISTMAS
from the Motion Picture Irving Berlin's HOLIDAY INN

Words and Music by
IRVING BERLIN
Arranged by Kevin Olson

© Copyright 1940, 1942 by Irving Berlin
Copyright Renewed
International Copyright Secured   All Rights Reserved

WINTER WONDERLAND

Words by DICK SMITH
Music by FELIX BERNARD
Arranged by Kevin Olson

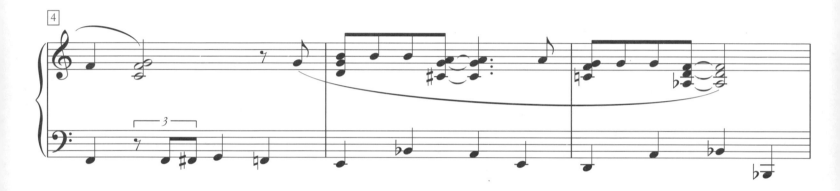

© 1934 (Renewed) WC MUSIC CORP.
All Rights for the Dick Smith share in Canada Administered by REDWOOD MUSIC LTD.
All Rights Reserved   Used by Permission

ABOUT THE ARRANGER

Kevin Olson is an active pianist, composer, and member of the piano faculty at Utah State University, where he has taught courses in piano literature, pedagogy, accompanying, music theory, commercial composition, and rock & roll history, among others. In addition to his collegiate teaching responsibilities, Kevin coordinates the piano program at Utah State University, and oversees the Utah State University Youth Conservatory, which provides weekly group and private piano instruction to over 150 pre-college community students. The National Association of Schools of Music has recently recognized the Conservatory as a model for pre-college piano instruction programs. Before teaching at Utah State, he was on the faculty at Elmhurst College near Chicago and Humboldt State University in northern California.

A native of Utah, Kevin began composing at age five. When he was twelve, his composition, "An American Trainride," received the Overall First Prize at the 1983 National PTA Convention at Albuquerque, New Mexico. Since then he has been a Composer-in-Residence at the National Conference on Keyboard Pedagogy, and has written music commissioned and performed by groups such as the Five Browns, American Piano Quartet, *Chicago a cappella*, the Rich Matteson Jazz Festival, Music Teachers National Association, the Festival for Creative Pianists, the American Festival Chorus & Orchestra, and several piano teacher associations around the country. He gives workshops and performances nationally and internationally, most recently in India, China, Canada, and the United Kingdom.

Kevin maintains a large piano studio, teaching students of a variety of ages and abilities. Many of the needs of his own piano students have inspired hundreds of published books and solos, written in a variety of levels and styles. For more information, visit **www.kevinolsonmusic.com**.